Contemporary American History:
The United States
since 1945

DEWEY W. GRANTHAM

D1011941

AMERICAN HISTORICAL ASSOCIATION

AHA PAMPHLETS

215

Contemporary American History:
The United States since 1945

DEWEY W. GRANTHAM

215 AHA PAMPHLETS

AMERICAN HISTORICAL ASSOCIATION

400 A Street, SE, Washington, D.C. 20003

DEWEY W. GRANTHAM is professor of history at Vanderbilt
University. He is a graduate of the University of Georgia and
received the Ph.D. degree from the University of North
Carolina, where he studied with Fletcher M. Green. His major
fields of interest are twentieth-century American history and the
history of the modern South. Before joining the Vanderbilt
department of history in 1952, he taught at North Texas State
College and the Woman's College of the University of North
Carolina. He was a Social Science Research Council faculty fellow in 1959 and a John Simon Guggenheim Memorial Foundation fellow in 1960, served as president of the Southern Historical
Association, 1966–67, and is currently on the board of editors of
the *American Historical Review*. His publications include *Hoke
Smith and the Politics of the New South* (Baton Rouge, 1958) and *The
Democratic South* (Athens, Ga., 1963). Among his edited works are
Theodore Roosevelt (Englewood Cliffs, 1971) and *The Political Status
of the Negro in the Age of FDR*, by Ralph J. Bunche (Chicago,
1973). His study of postwar America, *The United States since 1945:
The Ordeal of Power*, will be published late in 1975.

An earlier version of this pamphlet, entitled The United States since
1945, *appeared in 1968 in a series published by the Service Center for
Teachers of History, affiliated with the American Historical Association.
With the discontinuation of the Service Center, this series of AHA
Pamphlets has been devised to replace the older series. The pamphlet as it is
printed here has been entirely rewritten, and the bibliographical material
has been brought up to date.*

Standard Book Number: 0-87229-019-0
Library of Congress Catalog Card Number: 75-7883

Composed and printed at The William Byrd Press, Inc.
Richmond, Virginia 23228
Printed in the United States of America

Contemporary American History:
The United States since 1945

DEWEY W. GRANTHAM

From the vantage point of the 1970s, the years since 1945 constitute a new and in many respects revolutionary age in American history. "The gulf separating 1965 from 1943," the cultural anthropologist Margaret Mead has written, "is as deep as the gulf that separated the men who became builders of cities from Stone Age men."[1] The new era was ushered in by the Second World War, which dramatized the apocalyptic nature of modern society and pointed up the general cultural crisis of the twentieth century. The war led to the creation of a mighty military force, brought about a great mobilization of industry and other resources, banished unemployment and freed the economy from the grip of the depression, helped redefine the role of government, invoked new international policies, and changed the nation's social structure. The most compelling of all the contrasts with former times was the bomb. The explosion of the first atomic bomb in July 1945, in a remote New Mexico desert, cast its shadow over the entire postwar period.

Yet much of the past persisted in the years after 1945. Established institutions remained strong, and older attitudes and values demonstrated remarkable vitality. Although events after World War II overtook Americans with breath-taking speed, they were far less revolutionary than were developments in many other parts of the world. It was ironic that the United States, itself the product of

[1] Margaret Mead, *And Keep Your Powder Dry: An Anthropologist Looks at America* (2d ed.; New York, 1965), xxx.

3

a revolution, should have come, in a new age of national revolutions, to be viewed by many people in other countries as a conservative society, dedicated to the maintenance of the status quo. Nevertheless the postwar period in the United States, as elsewhere, was essentially an era of historical change, disruption, and discontinuity.

The problem of periodization inevitably concerns all students of history, for the element of time is a fundamental determinant of any identifiable pattern of social change. Obviously the last three decades are not all of a piece. The uniformities apparent from a bird's-eye view become, upon closer inspection, much more diversified by time and circumstance. For example, the 1950s witnessed a general revival of religion, while the next decade brought a massive assault on the structure of American religious institutionalism. Indeed, the second half of the 1960s may represent a sharp turning point in our recent history, for the United States during those years experienced what appeared to be a pronounced shift in moral, religious, and esthetic attitudes. But however broken and incoherent the shape of their overall development may have been, the postwar years had much in common. They also share a distinctive historiography, since virtually all historical accounts of the period have necessarily been written by persons alive at the time of the events they describe.

The growing recognition of contemporary history as a legitimate field is no doubt rooted in the acceleration of the rate of change—in the increase in the velocity of history. Despite the limitations that surround it, contemporary history offers an invaluable perspective. As John Lukacs has noted, "The person who, in one way or another, participated in the period which he is describing, who had some kind of a living contact with the people and the events he deals with, has a potentially . . . inestimable advantage over other observers." The contemporary historian is in a position to appreciate the popular inclinations of the time, to detect the real tendencies in the opinions and sentiments of the people, and to be conscious of the passions that move the participants in his account. He can also contribute to what Lukacs calls "the deepening of the personal consciousness of history."[2]

[2] John Lukacs, *Historical Consciousness; Or, The Remembered Past* (New York, 1968), 93, 97.

The task of the historian of the recent past is to place contemporary events in historical perspective or, one might say, to treat the present as history. This is no easy matter. It is still hard to see the broad shape of the postwar period, to understand how it is related to the prewar epoch, and to perceive the pattern of its evolution through time. One's view is inevitably affected by a large amount of present-mindedness. Yet, by attempting to organize and interpret the tumultuous years since 1945, we can engage in the process Felix Gilbert describes as "reconstructing a historical consciousness that integrates the present with the past."[3] And without some awareness of the complexity, ambiguity, and burden of the past, we will surely be ill prepared to deal with the kaleidoscopic present and the onrushing future.

The Economic and Social Context

Emerging from the depression that racked the nation in the prewar years, the United States entered the greatest and most sustained period of prosperity in its history. The passage from war to peace was difficult, but the economy did not revert to the hard times of the 1930s. Instead Americans enjoyed an almost uninterrupted boom that raised production figures, incomes, and standards of living to heights which would have been unbelievable a short time earlier. Despite several recessions the gross national product, in constant dollars, increased more than twice the rate of population growth. By 1960 the GNP had reached $500 billion, and within little more than another decade it had climbed to the trillion-dollar level. "It became clear to all the world," the economist Harold G. Vatter writes, "that the United States economy after mid-century was capable of producing enough to provide every man, woman, and child with a minimum-comfort level of living."[4] Although the postwar years were not a time of affluence for all Americans, the economy seemed to have reached a new maturity on the basis of the transforming effects of the New Deal, the Second World War, and several novel ingredients introduced after 1945.

The unaccustomed prosperity brought good jobs, business op-

[3] John Higham, with Leonard Krieger and Felix Gilbert, *History: The Development of Historical Studies in the United States* (Englewood Cliffs, 1965), 387.
[4] Harold G. Vatter, *The U.S. Economy in the 1950's: An Economic History* (New York, 1963), 1.

portunities, and social mobility. Postwar America, in Eric F. Goldman's colorful phrase, "was not so much settling down as it was settling upward."[5] Visual and statistical evidence alike confirmed the boast that the United States had created the highest standard of living in the history of mankind. Foreign visitors remarked that Americans seemed more prosperous each time they visited the United States. In the new "affluent society" the business world was drawn as if by a magnet to the needs and desires of the consumer. The consumer market not only spread into all manner of personal services but also came to encompass an endless array of durable goods. Americans spent increasing amounts of money for entertainment, recreation, and travel, and the far-flung consumer culture spawned a variety of new institutions such as gourmet food stores, art centers, record stores, and pet shops.

All levels of American society increased their incomes during and after the war, but the relative positions of the various income segments did not change a great deal. The top five per cent of the recipients got a little over twenty per cent of the national income in 1970, as compared to about thirty-three per cent in 1929. On the other hand, the poorest fifth of the population consistently obtained five per cent or less of the national income during the 1940s and after. In the late 1950s social critics began to point out the persistence of poverty in the United States. One of the writers who publicized its existence was Michael Harrington, who argued in *The Other America* that too much had been made of the country's affluence, since, by his count, something like one-fourth of all Americans were living in poverty. "The millions who are poor in the United States," he wrote, "tend to become increasingly invisible." Yet they were actually all around, not only in the back country of the Appalachian Mountains, but in the Negro slums of the big cities, among migrant workers in the West, among those everywhere who lacked a high school education, and among the millions of people over sixty-five who were trying to live on incredibly small incomes. As Harrington said, poverty in America "is a culture, an institution, a way of life."[6]

No aspect of the American economy was more prominent than the continuing trend toward large-scale corporate enterprise. By

[5] Eric F. Goldman, *The Crucial Decade—And After: America, 1945–1960* (New York, 1960), 47.
[6] Michael Harrington, *The Other America: Poverty in the United States* (New York, 1962), 2, 16.

mid-century giant corporations dominated almost every area of the nation's business. The emerging supercorporations were national and even international in operation, bureaucratic in organization, and increasingly diversified in the range of their products and services. Economic concentration clearly led to a decline in traditional competition, increased the incidence of "administered prices," and made for instability in the economy. According to John Kenneth Galbraith in *The New Industrial State* (1967), the huge corporation had achieved such dominance of American industry that it could control its environment and immunize itself from the discipline of the competitive market and all mechanisms of external control. Nevertheless a good deal of competition continued to exist in certain sectors of the economy, and some economists contended that a system of checks and balances operated to ensure a maximum of efficiency and justice in economic life. Small business enterprise did not disappear, though its role seemed to become less significant. In 1958 there were some five million individually owned businesses outside of farming, mining, and fishing in the United States, but eighty-five per cent of all employed persons were working for someone else—as compared with thirty-six per cent in 1900.

During the New Deal an interplay of powerful public and private groups had come to regulate the economy. The emergence of an industrial labor force into public recognition and organized strength constituted an important part of the changing character of American capitalism. Organized labor continued to grow in the postwar years, but by the fifties the movement had lost its momentum and the unions' share of the total labor force began to decline slightly. A change in public opinion and several legislative acts withdrew some of labor's key advantages. Organized labor's loss of vitality was also related to the changing structure of employment. Increasingly after mid-century new jobs in the labor market were being created in such tertiary areas as government and services rather than manufacturing, where some older industries were declining and automation was taking its toll of workers. The white-collar worker was difficult to organize, though the unions eventually began to make gains among such groups as retail clerks, teachers, and government employees. In addition to its loss of militancy, organized labor had become a central institution in the American economy.

Farmers also composed an important element in the political

economy of the postwar era. While agriculture in general did not fare as well as most other parts of the economy, the political influence of farm associations and agrarian spokesmen remained strong. Basic agricultural policies adopted during the period of the New Deal were perpetuated year after year, even though much controversy surrounded acreage controls and price supports. Although millions of farmers and agricultural workers fled the farms and the number of farms dropped precipitously, the "farm problem" remained, the paradoxical offspring of a technological revolution in agriculture and great numbers of small and inefficient farm units whose position in the farm economy was steadily made more untenable by that revolution.

Government, too, had come to play a vital role in the operation of American capitalism. Government aided business in many ways, and businessmen more and more looked upon public agencies as allies rather than adversaries. During World War II the federal government began to assume the financial risks of innovation in many areas of scientific research, and this support was expanded after 1945. A community of interests developed between the Pentagon and the corporations that received the bulk of the military procurement funds, and the defense contractors were frequently able to avoid competition or to secure payments for billion-dollar cost overruns, as in the case of Lockheed's C–5 transport plane. Although federal administrators made recurrent attempts through antitrust suits to halt the trend toward ever-greater economic concentration, their successes were limited. As a matter of fact, the public showed little interest in the concentration of control in the economy and could be stirred out of its apathy only by some dramatic evidence of corporate abuse, as in the disclosure to the Kefauver committee in the late 1950s of fantastic profits in the drug industry. Nevertheless the national government now played an indispensable part in the nation's mixed economy, not so much through stringent regulation as through fiscal and monetary policies, administrative procedures, and assistance to business enterprise by means of a wide range of programs and activities.

So expansive was the United States economy that the output of goods and services doubled and then redoubled during the postwar period. Although the prosperous years after 1961 brought the longest unbroken peacetime economic growth in American history, those years were followed by a time of economic troubles and mounting concern over future prospects. The rate of growth slowed, unemployment reached a relatively high level, and in the 1970s inflation became acute. Meanwhile the administrations in Washington attempted one curative procedure after another without noticeable effect. Faced with fuel crises, worried by pollution and threats to the environment, and frustrated by the problem of uncontrolled inflation, Americans in the seventies were more deeply worried about their economy than at any time since the depression-ridden thirties. It appeared likely in the mid-1970s that the United States, whose economy had become far more interdependent than ever before, was entering an era of painful readjustment.

The enormous growth of the economy and the pervasive influence of technology quickened the pace of social change at mid-century. The population proved to be extraordinarily expansive, increasing from 139.9 million in 1945 to more than 211 million in 1974. The great increase in population and other demographic shifts were basic factors in the evolution of American society after the war. By the mid-1950s, W. W. Rostow observed in 1957, America had become "a suburbanizing nation, increasingly at work in large bureaucracies, with a new security of employment, rising levels of welfare, rising standards of education and of intellectual sophistication, and an increased social and political homogeneity." In certain respects the nation's society had become more homogeneous, more stable, more conservative, and less divided by geography and national origin. As Irene and Conrad Taeuber wrote in 1971, "Ours has been an assimilative society, with geographic migrations and social and economic mobilities contributing to, if not creating, a plural society rather than a fragmented population."[7] Even so, the United States retained much of its ethnic and "racial" heterogeneity.

Americans had always been a people on the move, and in the postwar years the open road beckoned them as never before. Millions of Negroes and poor whites left the South for Northern cities

---

[7] W. W. Rostow, "The National Style," in Elting E. Morison, ed., *The American Style: Essays in Value and Performance* (New York, 1958), 291; Irene B. Taeuber and Conrad Taeuber, "People of the United States in the Twentieth Century: Continuity, Diversity, and Change," *Items*, 25 (1971): 18.

during the 1940s and 1950s, and the sunshine and warm climate of California, Florida, and the Southwest attracted a host of new residents to those regions. In the age of the automobile, the jet airliner, and the expense account, people traveled constantly for business and pleasure. One out of every five Americans changed his place of residence each year. This constant movement, coupled with increasing social mobility, contributed to the erosion of regional, class, and ethnic distinctions and to the nation's growing cultural homogeneity. But the consequences of these movements were also manifested in such social problems as the swelling ghettos of large cities, the disintegrated, uprooted families, and the mounting volume of crime.

Among the most notable features of this geographical mobility was the continued shift from farm to city, bringing with it a decline in rural population and the triumph of the city over the country in customs, manners, and habits of thought. The cities grew so rapidly that, as Constance McLaughlin Green pointed out several years ago, "all American social history had become in essence urban history."[8] The most remarkable characteristic of postwar urbanization was the suburban explosion. By mid-century the suburbs had begun to shape and increasingly to dominate American society. The suburban trend reflected the great increase that was simultaneously taking place in social mobility. Much of the young, active, and better-educated population left the older parts of the metropolis for suburbia. The growth of the suburbs encouraged the decay and disorganization of the great cities and tended to lock millions of nonwhite and other poor people in the urban ghettos.

Social mobility in the United States during the 1940s and 1950s was almost as conspicuous as the movement of people across the face of the land. While there was substantial working-class social mobility in this period, the most impressive economic and social leveling was the broadening of the middle class. The steady increase in per capita income, the vast changes in the structure of employment, and the great expansion in the number of college graduates all helped to swell the ranks of the middle class. A new popular culture was emerging, promoted, as Daniel Bell has written, by "the cultural absorption into American life of the children of

[8] Constance McLaughlin Green, *The Rise of Urban America* (New York, 1965), 178.

the immigrant generation; the *embourgeoisement* of the working class; the spread of suburbia; the increase of income—involving, in turn, a growing desire on the part of the lower middle class to live conspicuously well." One aspect of this mass culture, as Daniel J. Boorstin has suggested, was the part played by technological developments that have changed the "meaning of the moment" by "democratizing the repeatable experience."[9]

The extent to which political and economic power was monopolized in the postwar period has been a matter of considerable disagreement among social commentators and scholars. It was argued by many political scientists and other social analysts that a "pluralist" system had emerged in the United States, despite the trend toward economic concentration, bureaucracy, and centralized administration. Power in this system was dispersed among numerous voluntary associations or "veto groups," which balanced each other in a rough equilibrium. Other analysts contended that power was concentrated in the hands of economic and social elites. In *The Power Elite* (1956) the sociologist C. Wright Mills asserted that most people in the American political system were powerless and that a complex elite of political, business, and military leaders ruled the country. Mills stressed elite domination rather than class control, but in the 1960s several other writers began to emphasize class differentials and tensions in explaining the concentration of wealth and power in the United States.

If the middle register of the American social order was expanding, it also appeared to be increasingly homogenized. Americans, especially the white-collar employee and the suburban dweller, seemed to conform not only in dress, food, and housing, but even in their ideas. Novels such as Sloan Wilson's *The Man in the Gray Flannel Suit* (1956) and sociological studies like C. Wright Mills's *White Collar: The American Middle Classes* (1951) called attention to the loss of individuality, the stuffiness, and the mindless materialism that characterized much contemporary middle-class living. Machine industry and mass production, some observers noted in the 1950s, were leading to a cultural standardization on a fairly low level and to a loss of individual initiative. The psychologist Erich Fromm, for

---

[9] Daniel Bell, "Modernity and Mass Society: On the Varieties of Cultural Experience," in Arthur M. Schlesinger, jr. and Morton White, eds., *Paths of American Thought* (Boston, 1963), 415; Daniel J. Boorstin, *The Americans: The Democratic Experience* (New York, 1973), 359, 371.

instance, wrote of the prevalence of individuals with a "marketing orientation," individuals who wanted to avoid having to make choices and eagerly accepted values imposed by the group. David Riesman pointed to the way in which the consumer-oriented economy reinforced the old American tendency to conform to the tastes and attitudes of one's neighbors. Riesman suggested, in *The Lonely Crowd: A Study of the Changing American Character* (1950), that the national character had changed from an "inner-directed" type, responding to a sort of internal gyroscope, to an "other-directed" personality, basically attuned to the mass values of one's neighbors.

The social conformity that Riesman and other writers described—and probably exaggerated—was related to a widespread nostalgia for older values and a quest for security in the assumed certainty and stability of the old America. An extreme manifestation of this mood was McCarthyism, which, in part at least, was a product of new social anxieties. The so-called radical Right of the fifties and sixties seemed to fear not only communism but "modernity" as well, and thus to be alienated from contemporary society. The search for identity among the pressures of a plural but conformist society was a principal theme in the sociological studies of the postwar era. Thus Will Herberg, in *Protestant—Catholic—Jew: An Essay in American Religious Sociology* (1955), interpreted the increased religious activity of contemporary America as a way of maintaining group identity in a democratic society that frowned upon the maintenance of sharply differentiated national groups. Meanwhile, after a period of rising birth rates and preoccupation with domesticity that lasted through the 1950s, the American family began to show unprecedented signs of strain and instability. This was not the case with the voluntary association. In fact the voluntary group had become more than ever before the primary institution for maintaining American society or reforming it. People were likely to belong to voluntary associations of many types, and in a sense the family, the church, and the community were reduced to virtual subspecies of such organizations.

Political Patterns

The political scene was turbulent and uncertain during Harry S. Truman's presidency. Congress wanted to reassert its authority after the long years of executive dominance under Franklin D. Roosevelt. The Republicans, repeatedly frustrated by Roosevelt's party leadership, were impatiently waiting to resume control of the national government. Every interest group identified with the Democratic party, moreover, came out of the war with high hopes and expectations for the future, and the Truman administration quickly discovered that it was unable to move far in any direction without seeming to jeopardize the gains made by some important group of constituents. Postwar prosperity also weakened the force of economic liberalism. There was a certain ambiguity in the outlook of the new middle class, which was steadily absorbing portions of the "have-not" groups and urban masses attracted to the New Deal in the 1930s. While loyal to New Deal liberalism, on the one hand, these groups were, on the other, becoming more politically conservative. Although Truman won broad support for his foreign policies, his administration's preoccupation with the cold war inhibited domestic reforms and endangered civil liberties.

The early postwar elections proved indecisive. The elections of 1946 returned the Republicans to control of Congress for the first time in sixteen years, but Truman's startling victory in 1948 apparently demonstrated, if not the continuing vitality of the Democratic coalition, at least the determination of its principal components to preserve the gains of the New Deal. In spite of all its vicissitudes, the New Deal constituency held together reasonably well during the Truman years. Still, the politics of stalemate, evident as early as 1938, persisted, sustained by the powerful conservative coalition in Congress, the internal conflict within the majority party, and the ambivalence of the public mood. The Truman administration failed to achieve a break-through on the domestic front comparable to the radical new departure it introduced in the international sphere. Truman secured, however, additions to many New Deal programs, and in the Fair Deal he formulated a long-range agenda for liberal action.

Dwight D. Eisenhower's huge majority in 1952 apparently indicated the breakup of the Roosevelt coalition. Coming to office at a time of confusion, division, and bitterness, the immensely popular "Ike" rendered the politics of the 1950s less acrimonious, eased the tensions after a generation of crisis, and helped restore a sense of national unity. Eisenhower's restrained approach to government

13

and his moderate Republicanism blended comfortably into a national mood of complacency, well-being, and self-indulgence. Richard Rovere has suggested that, in part because he was a Republican, the thirty-fourth president was able to do "many of the things that needed doing and that could not have been done by a Democratic administration."[10] Thus he liquidated the Korean War without being called an appeaser and accepted the essential features of the Roosevelt "revolution," helping to consolidate it as the programmatic base of American politics. Yet the general did little to alter the static quality of the nation's politics, and he interpreted his mandate in domestic affairs as one of conservatism and slowing the pace of change.

The yearning for repose and the conservative temper began to change in the late 1950s. The Democrats, who regained control of Congress in 1954 and greatly strengthened their majorities in 1958, became more aggressive. During the second Eisenhower administration they began to develop new programs, draft remedial measures, and secure party commitment to such reform proposals. These developments laid the basis for what would ultimately become the New Frontier and the Great Society. Taking advantage of a cultural shift that had begun to spread through American society and identifying himself with the growing desire for a renewed sense of national purpose and a more dynamic government in Washington, John F. Kennedy narrowly won the presidency in 1960. Kennedy was the first Catholic to become president, and his election seemed to signal a reorientation of American politics. But he was unable to end the executive-legislative deadlock in Washington, even though his style and personality had a remarkable impact upon his contemporaries, particularly young people. His tragic death produced its own mythology, including the legend of Camelot, whose gallant king gave the nation a moment of glory before dying for its sins.

Making the most of Kennedy's martyrdom and associating himself with the goals of the New Frontier, Lyndon B. Johnson completed the enactment of his predecessor's reform measures and proceeded to sponsor the most advanced program of social reform in American history. For the first time in more than a quarter cen-

---

[10] Richard H. Rovere, "Eisenhower over the Shoulder," *American Scholar,* 31 (1962): 177.

tury the hold of the Southern Democratic-Republican coalition in Congress was broken. In the mid-1960s a spate of Great Society bills swept through the two houses on Capitol Hill. Johnson also created, momentarily, what he liked to consider a national political consensus. The consensus seemed to be evident in Johnson's landslide victory at the polls in 1964, a triumph produced by the president's record of accomplishments and the Republican party's venture into militant conservatism under the leadership of Senator Barry M. Goldwater. The senator's extremism alarmed and divided the Republican party, allowing Johnson to capture the political center.

Then, almost overnight it seemed, the Johnsonian consensus was disrupted and the Great Society lost its momentum. The dark forebodings aroused by John F. Kennedy's assassination in 1963 and the Watts riot of 1965 were realized with a vengeance in the social violence and conflict that characterized the following years. Johnson became increasingly preoccupied with the war in Vietnam, which provoked a far-reaching protest movement at home, tested the fundamental assumptions underlying American foreign policy, and encouraged a critical reappraisal of the nation's political institutions, culture, and values. The president's problems were complicated by what many Americans came to see as his duplicity—his "credibility gap." Frustrated and unable to govern effectively, Johnson suddenly announced, in March 1968, that he would not accept another nomination as his party's candidate for president. But by this time the Democratic party was riddled by schism. The ensuing struggle for the nomination, the murder of Robert F. Kennedy, and the bitter confrontations at the Democratic national convention in Chicago completed the party's disarray. The Democratic coalition was threatened both by the fragmentation of the political Left and by the defection of Southern whites and working-class Democrats, many of whom were attracted by the conservatism of Governor George C. Wallace.

Richard M. Nixon, the Republican nominee in 1968, took advantage of the divisions in the Democratic party and the spreading wave of reaction among millions of Americans. Like Eisenhower in 1952, Nixon promised to end the war in the Far East and to restore stability and unity to American society. Nixon's campaign was also designed to take advantage of the fact that race relations and crime and lawlessness, along with the Vietnam War, had become the major areas of public concern in the United States. Emphasizing what he called the "forgotten Americans," the Republican leader urged an end to violence and confrontations, the need for retrenchment and a re-examination of domestic welfare programs, and a commitment to the support of "law and order." His "Southern strategy" enabled him to divide the South with Wallace's American Independent party. The public sought out the "defensive middle ground" in 1968, and as David S. Broder says, the central paradox of the election is that, in a year of almost unprecedented violence, turmoil, and political oscillations, the electorate gave "a terribly conventional result."[11] Nixon's popular plurality was nevertheless only slightly larger than Hubert H. Humphrey's vote, and the election was one of the closest in modern United States history.

Although the Nixon administration catered to the fears and prejudices of the "silent majority," the Republicans lost the mid-term congressional elections of 1970 and approached the presidential election of 1972 with great apprehension. But they benefited from the strife-torn Democratic party and from Senator George S. McGovern's image as a candidate of the Left, as well as from the president's bold initiatives in foreign affairs. Despite the fact that Democrats continued to control Congress, Nixon's overwhelming electoral success in 1972 seemed to provide support for the idea of an emerging Republican majority. Republican hopes were quickly dashed, however, by the Watergate scandal, which dominated national politics in 1973 and 1974, forced President Nixon's resignation in the face of almost certain impeachment, and brought Gerald R. Ford to the White House in August 1974 as the nation's thirty-eighth president.

Several explosive issues came to the fore in the years after 1945, arousing deep emotions among the voters and cutting across the existing party structure. The Republican party, as the minority party, attempted to capitalize on these potentially realigning issues, while the majority Democrats, hoping to avoid realignment, usually emphasized the traditional economic and class-related issues that had served them well in the 1930s.

[11] David S. Broder, "Election of 1968," in Arthur M. Schlesinger, jr. and Fred L. Israel, eds., *History of American Presidential Elections, 1789–1968* (New York, 1971), 4: 3705.

Communism was the first of these major issues to develop following the war. In the late 1940s and early 1950s an exaggerated fear of internal subversion swept over the United States. Frustrated by their loss of the presidency in 1948 and encouraged by a series of shocking developments in 1949 and 1950, including the fall of Nationalist China and the Korean War, Republican leaders eagerly seized upon anticommunism as a partisan issue. In addition the race question emerged as a powerful political issue in the 1950s. It lent a new urgency to the problem of racial injustice, contributed to the coalescence of a new wave of social reform, and became the most immediate factor in the defection of the South from the classic Democratic coalition.

In the 1960s two other issues had a profound impact upon the nation's politics: Vietnam and the question of "law and order." The bitter conflict engendered by Lyndon B. Johnson's policies in Vietnam fragmented the Democratic party, promoted the rise of a new social radicalism in America, and made it possible for the Republicans to recapture the White House in 1968. The issue of "law and order"—what Richard M. Scammon and Ben J. Wattenberg have labeled "the social issue"[12]—was also employed to good effect by Republicans. Closely related to the race issue, "law and order" became code words that summed up the growing middle-class fear of violence and opposition to crime, ghetto riots, student disorders, and the national welfare system.

Although Dwight Eisenhower and Richard Nixon shattered the Democratic majority coalition in presidential elections, no major party realignment has occurred since the 1930s. The election of 1952 proved to be a deviation, and despite the remarkable majority registered for the Republican presidential ticket in 1972, the Democrats retained control of Congress and more than held their own in state and local elections. None of the issues of the postwar period produced a decisive political realignment, mainly, it appears, because they were not issues on which the major parties took distinct and opposing policy positions. In other words, the two parties have not differed much on basic policy objectives, but rather, as James L. Sundquist observes in *Dynamics of the Party System* (1973), on the selection and administration of the means to agreed-upon

[12] Richard M. Scammon and Ben J. Wattenberg, *The Real Majority* (New York, 1970), 20–21, 35–44.

ends. Only the race question, of the four disruptive issues cited here, still seems to offer some prospect as a realigning issue. Nevertheless all of these issues had a disrupting effect upon the Democratic party, and while the Democrats continued to get a majority of the total votes in national elections, many of their supporters became less firmly attached to the party than in earlier years. Indeed the movement of large numbers of voters from identification with either of the major parties to independence is one of the most pronounced trends in contemporary American politics. At least a third of the nation's voters now classify themselves as independents, and there is a great deal more ticket splitting than formerly.

Despite the fierce party battles and the polarizing effects of issues like communism in government and racial equality, a fundamental consensus prevailed in American political thought during the early postwar period. The relative success of the New Deal in creating a "balanced" society, along with the threat of totalitarianism before and after the war, promoted this consensus. The war itself, while weakening liberalism in some respects, encouraged a broad reaffirmation of American society and values. Liberals and conservatives now seemed less distinct, less separated by ideological differences. Following the war the Republican party accepted the essentials of the New Deal as well as the cold-war assumptions and containment policies of the Truman administration. Liberals assumed a militantly anti-Communist position and stressed what Arthur M. Schlesinger, jr. called "the vital center" in his book of that name (1949), a central doctrine midway between the totalitarian poles of fascism and communism. President Truman and other American liberals also stressed a new approach to economics—the notion of a continually expanding capitalist economy undergirded by Keynesian fiscal policies and an extensive social welfare program.

The widespread satisfaction with the American system was reflected in the work of the consensualist social scientists and historians who influenced the intellectual currents of the 1950s. Emphasizing the positive and functional side of existing institutions in the United States, they tended to assign a normative role to America's pluralistic, democratic capitalism. Some social theorists such as Daniel Bell even proclaimed "the end of ideology" in the economically mature democracies of the West, whose "open" and pluralistic societies had apparently avoided the dangers of philosophical absolutism and monolithic social structures.[13]

Momentarily, at the height of Johnson's Great Society, liberalism seemed on the verge of realizing its most cherished goals. But a time of crisis quickly followed, precipitated by the struggle in Vietnam but also reflecting the criticisms of earlier dissenters. "Something in the experience of many young men and women at the end of the 1950s," writes Irwin Unger, "had produced an altered consciousness that made for a critical, disapproving, and hostile view of American—and Western European—life and created a desire to change it in drastic ways."[14] By the mid-1960s the intellectual-political consensus was under sharp attack, and much of the criticism came from within the political Left. The growing awareness of poverty and racism in America, the sharpening perception of a military-industrial complex, and the endless and destructive war in Southeast Asia created mounting disillusionment, protest, and radical social critiques. A "New Left" took shape, calling attention to the shortcomings of the nation's pluralistic economy and challenging the accuracy of "pluralism" as a description of American society. By the early 1970s the New Left as a phenomenon of social relevance had gone into eclipse, its demise hastened by Nixon's foreign policy initiatives, Watergate, and daily concern over a runaway inflation. Perhaps cultural dissent will be the New Left's most lasting contribution. But in any case, the radical criticism of the late sixties was part of a broader reevaluation of American life, part of a moral and esthetic revolution that may constitute a watershed in our recent experience.

Revolutionary Themes

One avenue to an understanding of postwar America is to identify and evaluate the complex social changes that have swept through our society during the past three decades. The revolutionary spirit in this period has had many facets—technological, social and economic, political, and cultural. But among the multiple revolutions in American life since the end of the

---

[13] Daniel Bell, *The End of Ideology: On the Exhaustion of Political Ideas in the Fifties* (rev. ed.; New York, 1962).

[14] Irwin Unger, *The Movement: A History of the American New Left, 1959–1972* (New York, 1974), 29.

Second World War none was more portentous than the involvement of the United States with the rest of the world. Americans soon discovered that in the cold war it was virtually impossible to discuss domestic questions without referring to foreign affairs; almost every political issue was affected with a global interest. Geographically the nation's diplomatic concerns became far broader than ever before, and many new agencies and instruments were soon involved in the conduct of foreign relations.

Americans had begun to forsake their traditional isolationism in the late thirties. The Japanese attack on Pearl Harbor destroyed the old myth of American impregnability, and during the war the United States became the organizer and leader of the United Nations in destroying the Axis powers and establishing an international organization for peace. Most Americans thought that it was both possible and desirable for the United States to use its immense power to help reshape the world along the lines of its own democratic capitalism. A national consensus soon developed to support Washington's opposition to the Soviet Union in the cold war, which Americans viewed in terms of mortal combat between their own traditional ideals and moral judgments and a "totalitarian" system and an "evil" ideology. They were prepared to tolerate a long period of twilight between total war and total peace, a generation of almost unrelieved tension, repeated crises, and prolonged stalemate.

The revolution in American foreign policy was directly related, of course, to certain changes in the rest of the world. One such change was the decline of Europe's pre-eminence in world affairs, a development associated with the collapse of Western imperialism, the revolt of the peoples of Asia and Africa, the rise of Eastern nationalism, and the polarization of power between the United States and the Soviet Union. A second impetus to America's changing foreign policy was the end of what C. Vann Woodward has described as "the era of free security"—the physical security from hostile attack and invasion the country enjoyed through most of its history. The end of this era came so suddenly and swiftly that Americans could hardly bring themselves to face its practical implications.[15] A third factor in transforming the nation's foreign

[15] C. Vann Woodward, *The Age of Reinterpretation*, Service Center for Teachers of History series, 35 (Washington, 1961), 2–7.

policy was the revolution in weapons technology that began during World War II. Historic changes in weapons, tactics, and strategy were insignificant when contrasted with the distance separating the preatomic and the nuclear ages.

The bulwark of American foreign policy in the cold war was the doctrine of containment. First applied in 1947 when the Truman Doctrine was devised to counter the Russian attempt to make a major break-through in the eastern Mediterranean and the Marshall Plan was worked out to deal with the postwar crisis in Europe, containment was later extended to Asia and the Middle East. Tension between the two superpowers waxed and waned, but the United States steadily adhered to the containment rationale. The policy of deterrence was a companion of containment. In order to block Communist expansion, U.S. leaders insisted that the country must possess military power of such formidable proportions as to discourage or prevent any attempt by its adversaries to take territory by force. It is not surprising that the Russians made the same assumptions. A third American policy in the postwar period was aid to underdeveloped areas. It was assumed in the Marshall Plan and other programs that one way to fight communism was to use United States wealth to provide succor to the poor, the hungry, and the hopeless in non-Communist lands. Humanitarian considerations and an awareness of long-range economic benefits also motivated American policy makers. The most popular addition to foreign aid programs in the 1960s was the Peace Corps, which effectively combined youthful idealism and many forms of technical assistance.

President Truman's decisive action in sending American troops into battle in support of South Korea demonstrated that the United States would enforce its containment policy in the Far East as well as in Europe. But the Korean War put many aspects of the new foreign policy to the test, and after the Eisenhower administration ended the struggle with a compromise settlement in 1953, the focus of American concern in East Asia shifted to Indochina. The large-scale United States involvement in the Vietnam War that began in 1965 eventually brought about a partial repudiation of the containment doctrine. The rapprochement with Communist China and the détente with the Soviet Union arranged by President Nixon and Henry A. Kissinger attested to the fact that international affairs

21

were no longer dominated by the East-West conflict and the old cold-war suppositions. By the 1970s there were at least five great power centers—the United States, Russia, Western Europe, China, and Japan—and American leaders were searching for viable arrangements that would recognize the new realities. Opinion surveys in the early 1970s indicated that a growing percentage of Americans wanted their country to assume a more modest role in international affairs and that many people no longer considered it important for the United States to be "the world's most powerful nation." Vietnam also stimulated an attempt to curb presidential power in foreign policy, especially the power to commit troops to battle. The military establishment remained powerful, however, and "national security" continued to evoke broad public support.

Another revolutionary change in postwar America occurred in the position of the nation's largest minority group. Stimulated by the political ferment of the New Deal and by the economic advances and democratic slogans of the Second World War, Negro leaders and organizations in the late 1940s and early 1950s began more vigorously to assert their claim to equality and to protest their race's second-class status. The Truman administration committed itself to a broad civil rights program, and in 1954 the United States Supreme Court, in *Brown* v. *Board of Education of Topeka,* handed down an epochal decision that served to mobilize the energies of the black community and to give impetus to a great national reform movement. The role of the Supreme Court as an agent of change in race relations was the most conspicuous part of a far-reaching judicial revolution in the fifties and sixties embracing democratic and libertarian goals.

The civil rights movement soon entered into a more active phase in which new leaders, new organizations, and new tactics came to the fore. Having found a great symbolic leader in Martin Luther King, Jr. and a powerful tactic in the doctrine of nonviolent resistance, the equal rights movement gained still more impetus and achieved a new urgency. The federal government was drawn increasingly into the struggle, both by forcing compliance with desegregation court decisions, as at Little Rock, Arkansas, and Oxford, Mississippi, and in the passage of stronger laws. As public pressure mounted and the Kennedy and Johnson administrations mobilized their full resources in behalf of stronger legislation,

Congress finally responded, in 1964, with the enactment of a comprehensive Civil Rights Act that outlawed segregation in places of public accommodation and struck at other types of racial discrimination. In 1965 a sweeping voting rights law was adopted, and during the following year still other federal restrictions against racial discrimination were written into law. By the mid-1960s the "Second Reconstruction" had achieved far more than had the first Reconstruction almost a century earlier, leading C. Vann Woodward to conclude, in a revised edition of *The Strange Career of Jim Crow,* that a "national consensus" on the race issue "was in the making and a peaceful solution was in sight."[16]

But even as state-imposed segregation was being struck down there were signs that the black American's long quest for equality was still far from being won. Ironically the legal and political progress of the early sixties served to heighten black expectations, which all too often were not realized. Nothing revealed the growing mood of frustration, bitterness, and anger in the black community more dramatically than the explosion of ghetto riots between 1964 and 1968. By the middle of the decade the transformation of black protest from its emphasis on civil rights to what came to be called "black power" had already begun. Nonviolence as the guiding philosophy of black protest was increasingly challenged by black power. White and black attitudes were rapidly polarized, a "white backlash" began to manifest itself throughout the country, and "law and order" emerged as a key political issue. A variety of militant black leaders and organizations appeared, emphasizing black nationalism, self-determination through economic and political power, and the development of black pride and Afro-American culture.

Although racial tensions subsided somewhat as the political climate became less volatile in the early 1970s, the reality of racial inequality in America was still widely apparent. Yet a great social upheaval and a vast alteration had taken place in race relations in the United States in the postwar era. Equal rights for black Americans had become a momentous national issue, a new crisis in federalism had been precipitated, and the national government had mobilized its authority to destroy the legal structure of segregation and to combat racial discrimination in its many forms. The black

[16] C. Vann Woodward, *The Strange Career of Jim Crow* (2d rev. ed.; New York, 1966), 189.

revolution also served as a catalyst for other minority groups, which quickly began to emulate its organizations and tactics. The Chicano movement in the Mexican-American community, for instance, was based upon a deepening commitment to end discrimination against the members of that group and to uphold the values of cultural pluralism.

A third revolutionary theme in contemporary America is the "crisis of the cities." Somewhat paradoxically, the metropolis during the last three decades has been the dominating influence in American life while simultaneously sprawling far out into the surrounding countryside and being fragmented into scores of discrete population groupings. As the exodus from the central city to the mushrooming suburbs continued in the postwar years, most large cities were hard hit by the separation between the two regions. A whole range of social and human problems developed having to do with welfare, housing, education, transportation, crime, and the drug traffic. Much of the nation's social turmoil in the sixties and seventies was centered in its large cities, leading to talk of the "dying city." The urban crisis evoked extensive social analysis, and a great deal of energy and money was mobilized in reconstruction efforts, extending all the way from the activities of local governments and private organizations to federal programs like Johnson's Great Society.

Two other relatively new issues were related to the urban crisis. One of these was the sudden "discovery" of poverty in the midst of postwar affluence. Although millions of rural dwellers in contemporary America lived in poverty, the urban ghettos provided spectacular evidence of economically depressed elements. Thus the city slums were a major target of the federal government's war on poverty in the 1960s. The metropolitan areas were also a focal point of the growing environmental crisis. One reason for the rapid growth of the suburbs was the desire to escape from the congestion, noise, and pollution of the inner city and to find more space, clean air, and trees. Wherever they lived, Americans were increasingly aware of the fact that economic growth was accompanied by unwanted side effects, including a steady decline in the quality of the air and water, a series of man-made disasters of ecological imbalance, and widening alarm over the imminent destruction of the natural environment.

24

Still another manifestation of revolution in the postwar period was cultural in nature. An upheaval in American culture occurred in the late 1960s. This cultural revolution was evident in the emergence of a radical movement in politics, a counterculture led by young people, and a new morality that promoted a revolt against institutional unresponsiveness and hypocrisy, social inhumanity, and depersonalized life-styles. The protest against the Vietnam War triggered much of this dissent, but its roots reached down to more fundamental conditions such as the enormous strain placed on existing institutions by population growth and rapid technological change, the dominance of giant organizations in government, industry, labor, and education, and the pervasive feeling of impotence and powerlessness that overcame modern man. According to Theodore Roszak in *The Making of a Counter Culture* (1969), the cultural rebellion of youth was fundamentally a revolt against the dehumanizing effect of scientific and technological values and against an increasingly impersonal and bureaucratic society and in favor of the New Left's participatory democracy. The students who attacked the military-industrial complex in the late 1960s were rebelling against the anonymity of contemporary society and the impersonality and bureaucracy of the multiversities, the government, and virtually every important social institution. The student insurgence, the development of a counterculture, and the women's liberation movement all demonstrated in one way or another the search for new forms of community in a swiftly changing society.

The crisis of confidence that overtook Americans in the late sixties and early seventies mirrored a remarkable change in national outlook. A profound crisis of the spirit had settled over America, accompanied by a deep-seated pessimism unknown in the United States since the depths of the Great Depression. A series of enervating events contributed to this sense of foreboding. The energy crisis of the 1970s evoked the image of an economic "catastrophe," and the growing importance of ecological issues reflected the alarming realization that the quality of life itself might be worsening. The experience of the United States in Vietnam, more than any other aspect of the nation's recent history, demonstrated the limits of American power, destroyed a large part of the public's confidence in the country's capacity to deal with foreign and domestic

problems, and bruised the national spirit as had no other development in the twentieth century. Then came Watergate, which made
Americans acutely aware of the fragility of their political institutions and deepened the doubts that had already entered the public
consciousness. But the malaise went deeper still, to fundamental
questions like the sanctity of work, the stability of the family, and
the threat to such "familiar totems" as premarital chastity, the
postponement of gratification, and filial gratitude for parental
sacrifice.

The years after 1945 also dealt harshly with some of our national
myths—with such illusions as America's uniqueness, moral
superiority, invincibility, and inevitable success. Americans had
long thought of themselves as a chosen people, as what Paul Varg
has described as "the model republican society that the rest of the
world would emulate."[17] Such assumptions died hard, but in a new
age of revolution they could no longer be sustained with widespread
confidence. Still, few Americans were inclined to adopt a fatalistic
outlook. Somehow they could not share the attitude of Daniel
Patrick Moynihan, one of Kennedy's New Frontiersmen. When the
young president was struck down in Dallas, Moynihan stood the
shock better than most, remarking simply, "I don't think there's
any point in being Irish if you don't know that the world is going to
break your heart eventually."[18] Most Americans yearned for a hap-
py ending, or at least for the promise of one. We Americans,
observes Professor Woodward, have characteristically sought our
identity in the future. Perhaps we still do, and like F. Scott
Fitzgerald's Gatsby believe in the "future that year by year recedes
before us." "It eluded us then," Fitzgerald wrote at the end of *The
Great Gatsby,* "but that's no matter—tomorrow we will run faster,
stretch out our arms farther. . . . And one fine morning—"

Historiographical Perspectives

Scholarly inquiry into United States history
since 1945 is still in an early stage. The character of the Truman
period has been marked out in our recent political history, the
nature of postwar foreign policy has been probed, and the civil

[17] Paul A. Varg, *Foreign Policies of the Founding Fathers* (East Lansing, 1963), 303.
[18] Quoted in William L. O'Neill, *Coming Apart: An Informal History of America in the 1960's*
(Chicago, 1971), 93.

rights movement has been elucidated by historians and other scholars. Otherwise the history of the last three decades remains in large part *terra incognita*. There are as yet relatively few historical monographs and virtually no large-scale syntheses for the postwar era. Much of the literature that exists is understandably impressionistic, lacking in historical depth, and weak in analytical techniques. Even though the new interest in black history and the history of other neglected minorities has stimulated and broadened historical research, the best of this work has tended to focus on earlier periods.

For much that has happened in the recent past one must rely on the explosion of "instant" social history, social commentary, and eyewitness accounts sparked by postwar events. Writings in this genre are rarely satisfactory as history, but they are often valuable not only for their reconstruction of what happened but also for their assessment of the impact of motivating forces and the role of public opinion. Theodore H. White's *The Making of the President, 1960* (1961) is an example of a vivid eyewitness account that is well worth reading by anyone interested in contemporary American history. Books by participants are sometimes essential. Thus Dean Acheson's sprightly *Present at the Creation: My Years in the State Department* (1969) throws light on the foreign policy of the Truman administration. The two volumes of George F. Kennan's *Memoirs, 1925–1963* (1967–72) are a contribution both to the historiography of the cold war and to an understanding of decision making in recent U.S. foreign policy.

Some of the work of social scientists is even more valuable in reconstructing contemporary American history. Sociologists and other social scientists have often written the first scholarly interpretations of the recent past, though their primary object has usually been to analyze the nature of modern society. These studies also frequently compare contemporary phenomena with those of earlier periods. Social science investigations into such areas as urban problems, race relations, and the environmental crisis illuminate recent history, as do analyses of contemporary voting behavior, legislative action, economic development, and demographic trends. Historians have also been influenced by the ideas, concepts, and methods of the social sciences, and developments in those disciplines have brought them closer to various public policy concerns and stimulated their interest in interdisciplinary research.

The exigencies of the Second World War and the onset of the cold war encouraged a broad sympathy for the American past among historians. The early historical accounts of the postwar period reflected this conservative view, leading in the 1950s to a "consensus" emphasis upon the uniformities in our national life. Historical writings on the recent past also mirrored a broader interest in a new institutional approach and an organizational synthesis that focused upon social systems which increasingly defined and gave meaning to the lives of Americans. Finally, the radical revisionism of the 1960s had a telling impact on the historiography of the postwar era. The historians of the New Left condemned the cold war, distrusted established groups, opposed the "old politics," and began to elaborate a critical analysis of traditional American liberalism. They were intent upon creating a "new" past that would lend support to their analysis of contemporary society and politics. Responding to the events of the 1960s, the revisionists helped promote historical inquiry into such fields as black history and the reinterpretation of the cold war.

As might be expected, the Truman administration has been the subject of more historical study than any other part of the postwar era. The Truman presidency attracted historians not only because of the availability of many of its sources but also because numerous social and political crises after mid-century first became visible during that period. The substantial extent of the historical scholarship on the Truman years was revealed in a book edited by Richard S. Kirkendall in 1967 entitled *The Truman Period as a Research Field*. A sequel to this volume—*The Truman Period as a Research Field: A Reappraisal, 1972* (1974)—consisted of a set of conflicting interpretations of the Truman administration. It showed, in addition to the continuing progress of historical research and writing on the period, the impact of revisionist scholarship on its historiography, including what one contributor described as the "demythologizing tone" of recent Truman literature. Most important, perhaps, was the evidence these two volumes provided of solid monographs and specialized studies in such areas as agriculture, labor, housing, veterans' affairs, congressional action, civil rights, internal security, and foreign policy.

28

Gaddis Smith has pointed out that the historian dealing with American foreign relations since the end of World War II confronts three special problems: the size and complexity of the subject; the diversity, immensity, and partial inaccessibility of sources; and the "distorting impact" of the Vietnam War on the perceptions of both the interpreter and his students.[19] But these handicaps have not deterred scholars from entering into the field of postwar American diplomacy, and in fact no other aspect of recent United States history has been quite so extensively investigated. Much of the early postwar work in diplomatic history was carried out by the so-called power realism school—historians and political scientists such as George F. Kennan, Hans Morgenthau, and Robert E. Osgood. They tended to be critical of United States policy on the grounds that it was too often moralistic, legalistic, and inflexible, and that it thereby sacrificed the national interest. A more thoroughgoing group of revisionists began to emerge in the early 1960s.

One of the most influential members of this group was William Appleman Williams, who as early as 1959 published *The Tragedy of American Diplomacy,* a wide-ranging reinterpretation that explained United States foreign policy as largely the result of a conscious, ideological commitment to open-door expansion. Most of the New Left historians in later years stressed economic factors instead of ideology in explaining American expansion. But they were all inclined to view the American past as discreditable and in need of revising. They have been primarily interested in the origins of the cold war and in the American involvement in Vietnam. The New Left analysis of Vietnam contrasts both with the official interpretation and with a liberal dissenting one that pictured the American entrapment as an honest but tragic mistake. Radical revisionist histories concentrated on American behavior to the neglect of what was happening in other countries, were frequently present-minded in projecting current fears and frustrations onto history, and exaggerated the impact of economic forces on decision making while slighting the interplay of domestic politics and public opinion in the formulation of U.S. foreign policies. Nevertheless New Left

[19]Gaddis Smith, "The United States in World Affairs since 1945," in William H. Cartwright and Richard L. Watson, Jr., eds., *The Reinterpretation of American History and Culture* (Washington, 1973), 543.

interpretations provided a useful antidote to the generally admiring view of American policy held by many diplomatic historians.

All of these interpretive emphases have enriched our perceptions of the period since 1945. Although the great expanse of our contemporary history—from the 1950s on—is just beginning to be intensively studied by historians, the embryonic historiography of the postwar era is dynamic, controversial, and increasingly complex. It is clearly a part of the larger reinterpretation of American history that is now under way.

The books referred to in the following commentary represent only a selection from the large body of literature dealing with the years after 1945. The intent in this bibliographical essay is to cite the best historical studies of the period and to sample the most useful works on postwar themes by social scientists and popular interpreters. For more extensive listings students should consult these bibliographical guides: E. David Cronon and Theodore D. Rosenof, eds., *The Second World War and the Atomic Age, 1940–1973* (Northbrook, Ill., 1975); Frank Freidel and Richard K. Showman, eds., *Harvard Guide to American History* (rev. ed.; Cambridge, Mass., 1974); and William H. Cartwright and Richard L. Watson, Jr., eds., *The Reinterpretation of American History and Culture* (Washington, 1973), especially the essays by Richard S. Kirkendall and Gaddis Smith.

Although the period since 1945 still awaits its general historian, several comprehensive and authoritative textbooks are available, including Arthur S. Link and William B. Catton, *American Epoch: A History of the United States since 1900*, vol. 3: *The Era of the Cold War, 1946–1973* (4th ed.; New York, 1974); Ralph F. de Bedts, *Recent American History: 1945 to the Present* (Homewood, Ill., 1973); Paul K. Conkin and David Burner, *A History of Recent America* (New York, 1974); and Lawrence S. Wittner, *Cold War America: From Hiroshima to Watergate* (New York, 1974). William E. Leuchtenburg's *A Troubled Feast: American Society since 1945* (Boston, 1973) offers a fresh and perceptive interpretation of recent domestic history, while John Brooks's *The Great Leap: The Past Twenty-Five Years in America* (New York, 1966) is a lively social history. Howard Zinn, *Postwar America: 1945–1971* (Indianapolis, 1973), is a radical critique of U.S. foreign policy, race relations, politics, and the military-industrial complex.

Eric F. Goldman's dramatic and entertaining *The Crucial Decade—And After: America, 1945–1960* (New York, 1960) captures the excitement and summarizes the basic attitudes of a troubled decade, which the author sees as a definable epoch in recent American history. Herbert Agar, *The Price of Power: America since 1945* (Chicago, 1957), is less successful in explaining the same period. Ronald Berman's *America in the Sixties: An Intellectual History* (New York, 1968) is important for the 1960s, while William L. O'Neill's *Coming Apart: An Informal History of America in the 1960's* (Chicago, 1971) provides a critical perspective on the sixties and evokes much of the decade's fervor, hope, and anxiety.

The characteristics of the postwar economy are delineated in Harold G. Vatter's valuable book, *The U.S. Economy in the 1950's: An Economic History*

(New York, 1963). Vatter does a workmanlike job in analyzing the evolution of the economy and in judging its accomplishments and weaknesses. Thomas C. Cochran, *American Business in the Twentieth Century* (Cambridge, Mass., 1972), is a thoughtful synthesis of modern American business history. Alfred D. Chandler's *Strategy and Structure: Chapters in the History of the Industrial Enterprise* (Cambridge, Mass., 1962) is especially valuable for the emergence of the great multidivisional, decentralized, and bureaucratized industrial firm. Other good studies of the role of the modern corporation are Robert T. Averitt, *The Dual Economy: The Dynamics of American Industry Structure* (New York, 1968), an original treatment of the big corporation in contemporary America, and Robert Sobel, *The Age of Giant Corporations: A Microeconomic History of American Business, 1914–1970* (Westport, Conn., 1972), a general account with good chapters on the rise and decline of the conglomerate movement. Two specific industries in the post-1945 period are described in Lawrence J. White, *The Automobile Industry since 1945* (Cambridge, Mass., 1971), and John B. Rae, *Climb to Greatness: The American Aircraft Industry, 1920–1960* (Cambridge, Mass., 1968).

Federal fiscal policy and the role of government in the postwar economy are the subjects of several notable books. *The Fiscal Revolution in America* (Chicago, 1969) by Herbert Stein is a first-rate study of the development of the "new economics" and of fiscal policies since the New Deal. Edward S. Flash, Jr., *Economic Advice and Presidential Leadership: The Council of Economic Advisers* (New York, 1965), is also illuminating on economic issues and administration policies, as is A. E. Holmans, *United States Fiscal Policy, 1945–1959: Its Contribution to Economic Stability* (London, 1961). Jim F. Heath, *John F. Kennedy and the Business Community* (Chicago, 1969), and Hobart Rowen, *The Free Enterprisers: Kennedy, Johnson, and the Business Establishment* (New York, 1964), are useful for the 1960s. Walter Adams and Horace M. Gray are critical of the relationship between government and business in their *Monopoly in America: The Government as Promoter* (New York, 1955), while Bernard D. Nossiter criticizes the liberal economics and attacks the validity of the theory of countervailing power in *The Mythmakers: An Essay on Power and Wealth* (Boston, 1964).

There is not an adequate social history of the United States after 1945, although Rowland Berthoff provides a good background in *An Unsettled People: Social Order and Disorder in American History* (New York, 1971). Max Lerner's *America as a Civilization: Life and Thought in the United States Today* (New York, 1957) is a broad social commentary packed with information on the first postwar decade. Informative descriptions of American society based on census data are contained in Ben J. Wattenberg and Richard M. Scammon, *This U.S.A.: An Unexpected Family Portrait of 194,067,296*

Americans, Drawn from the Census (Garden City, 1965), and Wattenberg, *The Real America: A Surprising Examination of the State of the Union* (Garden City, 1974). A comprehensive compilation of what contemporary Americans are thinking is provided by Frank E. Armbruster and Doris Yokelson in *The Forgotten Americans: A Survey of Values, Beliefs, and Concerns of the Majority* (New Rochelle, 1972). The continuing geographical mobility of Americans is highlighted in Vance O. Packard's popular work, *A Nation of Strangers* (New York, 1972). The persistence of regionalism is revealed in John Shelton Reed, *The Enduring South: Subcultural Persistence in Mass Society* (Lexington, Mass., 1972), and Thomas D. Clark, *The Emerging South* (2d ed.; New York, 1968).

The sociologist Milton M. Gordon is the author of a valuable book on ethnic group relations entitled *Assimilation in American Life: The Role of Race, Religion, and National Origins* (New York, 1964). Gordon summarizes three contending ideologies and shows that ethnic and religious differences continue to persist. Additional evidence of the continuing diversity of American society and culture can be found in Gerhard E. Lenski, *The Religious Factor: A Sociological Study of Religion's Impact on Politics, Economics, and Family Life* (Garden City, 1961); Nathan Glazer and Daniel Patrick Moynihan, *Beyond the Melting Pot: The Negroes, Puerto Ricans, Jews, Italians, and Irish of New York City* (Cambridge, Mass., 1963); and Michael Novak, *The Rise of the Unmeltable Ethnics: Politics and Culture in the Seventies* (New York, 1972).

Peter M. Blau and Otis Dudley Duncan, *The American Occupational Structure* (New York, 1967), is a good analysis of U.S. social structure. The persisting gap between income classes is shown in Gabriel Kolko, *Wealth and Power in America: An Analysis of Social Class and Income Distribution* (New York, 1962), and Robert J. Lampman, *The Share of Top Wealth-Holders in National Wealth, 1922–56* (Princeton, 1962). Morton Mintz and Jerry S. Cohen argue in *America, Inc.: Who Owns and Operates the United States* (New York, 1971) that American wealth and economic power are being increasingly concentrated in giant corporations. The rich and the poor are delineated in Ferdinand Lundberg, *The Rich and the Super-Rich: A Study in the Power of Money Today* (New York, 1968); Michael Harrington, *The Other America: Poverty in the United States* (New York, 1962); Herman P. Miller, *Rich Man, Poor Man* (New York, 1964); and Richard L. Morrill and Ernest H. Wohlenberg, *The Geography of Poverty in the United States* (New York, 1971).

The postwar years brought increasing evidence of a trend toward mass society and cultural standardization. Such well-known sociological studies as *The Lonely Crowd: A Study of the Changing American Character* (New Haven, 1950) by David Riesman and associates and *The Organization Man* (New

York, 1956) by William H. Whyte emphasize the tendency toward a coercive conformity in contemporary America and the psychological toll exacted by social change. A careful work by Arthur J. Vidich and Joseph Bensman, *Small Town in Mass Society: Class, Power, and Religion in a Rural Community* (Princeton, 1958), shows that despite the myth of local autonomy, every aspect of village life depends upon adjusting to mass society. The growing importance of popular culture is discussed in Philip Olson, *America as a Mass Society: Changing Community and Identity* (New York, 1963); Alvin Toffler, *The Culture Consumers: A Study of Art and Affluence in America* (New York, 1964); and Russel B. Nye, *The Unembarrassed Muse: The Popular Arts in America* (New York, 1970).

Samuel Lubell's classic work, *The Future of American Politics* (3d ed. rev.; New York, 1965), offers a provocative analysis of Franklin D. Roosevelt's political revolution, of the voting coalition he brought together, and of how, "after twenty years of victories, the coalition became deadlocked within itself." In *The Deadlock of Democracy: Four-Party Politics in America* (Englewood Cliffs, 1963) James MacGregor Burns argues that the political stalemate in the postwar era was rooted in the four-party system—each political party having a congressional and a presidential faction. James L. Sundquist's comprehensive historical analysis, *Dynamics of the Party System: Alignment and Realignment of Political Parties in the United States* (Washington, 1973), contains an enlightening discussion of national politics since 1945. Less historical but of great interest is Richard F. Hamilton, *Class and Politics in the United States* (New York, 1972). Among many books on recent presidents and presidential power, the most useful for the student of contemporary history are Walter Johnson, *1600 Pennsylvania Avenue: Presidents and the People, 1929–1959* (Boston, 1960); Elmer E. Cornwell, Jr., *Presidential Leadership of Public Opinion* (Bloomington, 1965); Richard E. Neustadt, *Presidential Power: The Politics of Leadership* (rev. ed.; New York, 1968); and Emmet John Hughes, *The Living Presidency: The Resources and Dilemmas of the American Presidential Office* (New York, 1973).

Theodore J. Lowi makes a critical and thoughtful examination of American political assumptions since the New Deal in *The End of Liberalism: Ideology, Policy, and the Crisis of Public Authority* (New York, 1969). Daniel Bell's *The End of Ideology: On the Exhaustion of Political Ideas in the Fifties* (rev. ed.; New York, 1962) is an important book. Edward A. Purcell, Jr., *The Crisis of Democratic Theory: Scientific Naturalism and the Problem of Value* (Lexington, Ky., 1973), is valuable for recent American political thought. Jerome M. Mileur, ed., *The Liberal Tradition in Crisis: American Politics in the Sixties* (Lexington, Mass., 1974), is a helpful anthology.

The presidential elections through 1968 are individually described in the fourth volume of Arthur M. Schlesinger, jr. and Fred L. Israel, eds.,

History of American Presidential Elections, 1789–1968 (New York, 1971), a work that includes contemporary documents and election figures. Volume 4 of another work edited by Schlesinger, *History of U.S. Political Parties* (New York, 1973), covers the period from 1945 to 1972. An invaluable collection of election data on the postwar period has been assembled by Richard M. Scammon, *America Votes: A Handbook of Contemporary American Election Statistics* (New York, 1956–72). The shifting pattern of voting behavior among socioeconomic groups is analyzed in V. O. Key, Jr., *The Responsible Electorate: Rationality in Presidential Voting, 1936–1960* (Cambridge, Mass., 1966). A slender volume based upon careful use of aggregate voting statistics and survey research data, this book suggests that the American electorate was "moved by concern about central and relevant questions of public policy, of governmental performance, and of executive personality" more than by irrational and sinister forces. Among the best popular accounts of postwar presidential elections are Theodore H. White's four volumes, *The Making of the President* (New York, 1961–73).

There are many good state and regional studies of political trends in the recent period. Examples of the former are James R. Soukup and others, *Party and Factional Division in Texas* (Austin, 1964); Numan V. Bartley, *From Thurmond to Wallace: Political Tendencies in Georgia, 1948–1968* (Baltimore, 1970); and Michael Paul Rogin and John L. Shover, *Political Change in California: Critical Elections and Social Movements, 1890–1966* (Westport, Conn., 1970). Change and continuity in Southern politics can be measured in V. O. Key, Jr., *Southern Politics in State and Nation* (New York, 1949), and William C. Havard, ed., *The Changing Politics of the South* (Baton Rouge, 1972).

Although there is not yet a satisfactory overall treatment of the Truman administration, Cabell Phillips, *The Truman Presidency: The History of a Triumphant Succession* (New York, 1966), is a useful work written from a "journalistic perspective." The most illuminating study of Truman's leadership as a liberal is Alonzo L. Hamby, *Beyond the New Deal: Harry S. Truman and American Liberalism* (New York, 1973), a balanced and judicious appraisal. Clifton Brock, *Americans for Democratic Action: Its Role in National Politics* (Washington, 1962), deals with a significant development in postwar liberalism. Of the Truman biographies the most adequate is Alfred Steinberg's *The Man from Missouri: The Life and Times of Harry S. Truman* (New York, 1962), a popular and admiring work. Barton J. Bernstein, the leading revisionist of Truman's domestic leadership, has edited an important collection of essays entitled *Politics and Policies of the Truman Administration* (Chicago, 1970). Another group of essays, more favorable toward Truman, is Alonzo L. Hamby, ed., *Harry S. Truman and the Fair Deal* (Lexington, Mass., 1974). The best general work of a documentary nature is Barton J. Bernstein and Allen J. Matusow, eds., *The Truman Administration: A Documentary History* (New York, 1966). Truman states his own case in his *Memoirs* (Garden City, 1955–56). An indispensable source of presidential messages, speeches, and statements for the period after 1945 is the *Public Papers of the Presidents of the United States* (Washington, 1958–). Another good reference work for the postwar era is *Congress and the Nation, 1945–1964: A Review of Government and Politics in the Postwar Years* (Washington, 1965) by the Congressional Quarterly Service. Two supplemental volumes have extended the coverage into the early 1970s.

The best-researched historical studies of the Truman administration have made good use of the materials in the Truman Library. These scholarly monographs include, in addition to Hamby's study, Richard O. Davies, *Housing Reform during the Truman Administration* (Columbia, Mo., 1966); Susan M. Hartmann, *Truman and the 80th Congress* (Columbia, Mo., 1971); Richard M. Dalfiume, *Desegregation of the U.S. Armed Forces: Fighting on Two Fronts, 1939–1953* (Columbia, Mo., 1969); Allen J. Matusow, *Farm Policies and Politics in the Truman Years* (Cambridge, Mass., 1967); R. Alton Lee, *Truman and Taft-Hartley: A Question of Mandate* (Lexington, Ky., 1966); Allen Yarnell, *Democrats and Progressives: The 1948 Presidential Election as a Test of Postwar Liberalism* (Berkeley, 1974); and William Howard Moore, *The Kefauver Committee and the Politics of Crime, 1950–1952* (Columbia, Mo., 1974). Stephen K. Bailey's *Congress Makes a Law: The Story behind the Employment Act of 1946* (New York, 1950) provides a revealing picture of the role played by various interest groups and organizations in the enactment of Public Law 304. An impressive study by Elmo Richardson, *Dams, Parks and Politics: Resource Development and Preservation in the Truman-Eisenhower Era* (Lexington, Ky., 1973), focuses on the Interior Department. Donald R. McCoy and Richard T. Ruetten, *Quest and Response: Minority Rights and the Truman Administration* (Lawrence, Kan., 1973), is the most thoroughly researched and broadly conceived book on civil rights during the Truman period. But see also the critical assessment by William C. Berman, *The Politics of Civil Rights in the Truman Administration* (Columbus, 1970).

There are still only a handful of first-rate biographies of postwar political leaders. James T. Patterson, *Mr. Republican: A Biography of Robert A. Taft* (Boston, 1972), is an unusually able treatment. Other superior biographies are Joseph Bruce Gorman, *Kefauver: A Political Biography* (New York, 1971); Norman D. Markowitz, *The Rise and Fall of the People's Century: Henry A. Wallace and American Liberalism, 1941–1948* (New York, 1973); and F. Ross Peterson, *Prophet without Honor: Glen H. Taylor and the Fight for American Liberalism* (Lexington, Ky., 1974).

If the cold war dominated the Truman administration's foreign policy decisions, the Communist issue within the United States rapidly emerged as a dangerous and explosive domestic concern. Earl Latham, *The Communist Controversy in Washington: From the New Deal to McCarthy* (Cambridge, Mass., 1966), contains a comprehensive discussion of the emergence of this issue, which is explained in terms of a conservative drive for power. Alan D. Harper, *The Politics of Loyalty: The White House and the Communist Issue, 1946–1952* (Westport, Conn., 1969), is a balanced treatment of the Truman administration's loyalty program. Richard M. Freeland, *The Truman Doctrine and the Origins of McCarthyism: Foreign Policy, Domestic Politics, and Internal Security, 1946–1948* (New York, 1972), contends that the administration prepared the way for McCarthyism by launching an anti-Communist propaganda offensive to win support for the Marshall Plan. The most notorious of the conspiracy cases, that of Alger Hiss, is vividly reported by Alistair Cooke, *A Generation on Trial: U.S.A. v. Alger Hiss* (2d ed.; New York, 1952). David A. Shannon traces the downhill path of the Communist party in *The Decline of American Communism: A History of the Communist Party of the United States since 1945* (New York, 1959). Walter Goodman, *The Committee: The Extraordinary Career of the House Committee on Un-American Activities* (New York, 1968), is useful for this era.

The senatorial stage is the focus of a fine book by Robert Griffith entitled *The Politics of Fear: Joseph R. McCarthy and the Senate* (Lexington, Ky., 1970). Griffith emphasizes political factors in his interpretation of McCarthyism. Michael Paul Rogin's *The Intellectuals and McCarthy: The Radical Specter* (Cambridge, Mass., 1967) is an impressive analysis of social theory, stressing the role of political elites in the development of McCarthyism. Richard H. Rovere, *Senator Joe McCarthy* (New York, 1959), is a perceptive character study. For civil liberties in the time of McCarthy, see Donald J. Kemper, *Decade of Fear: Senator Hennings and Civil Liberties* (Columbia, Mo., 1965); Milton R. Konvitz, *Expanding Liberties: Freedom's Gains in Postwar America* (New York, 1966); and Thomas C. Reeves, *Freedom and the Foundation: The Fund for the Republic in the Era of McCarthyism* (New York, 1969). In *The New American Right* (New York, 1955) and *The Radical Right: The New American Right Expanded and Updated* (Garden City, 1963) Daniel Bell and other scholars contend that McCarthyism and similar manifestations of extremism in contemporary politics can be explained in terms of "status anxieties" and tensions in American society. Seymour Martin Lipset and Earl Raab, *The Politics of Unreason: Rightwing Extremism in America, 1790–1970* (New York, 1970), is valuable for its analysis and perspective.

The first scholarly appraisal of the Eisenhower administration was Herbert S. Parmet's *Eisenhower and the American Crusades* (New York, 1972), a solid and judicious study that portrays Eisenhower as an astute and worthy president. Another useful work is Robert L. Branyan and

Lawrence H. Larsen, *The Eisenhower Administration, 1953–1961: A Documentary History* (New York, 1971), which is helpful in illuminating the political structure of the 1950s. For a useful collection of contemporary appraisals, see Dean Albertson, ed., *Eisenhower as President* (New York, 1963). The best biography of the thirty-fourth president is Peter Lyon's *Eisenhower: Portrait of the Hero* (Boston, 1974). Eisenhower's own comprehensive narrative of events was published as *The White House Years* (Garden City, 1963–65). Of the several personal accounts by members of the Eisenhower administration the best are Arthur Larson, *Eisenhower: The President Nobody Knew* (New York, 1968), and Emmet John Hughes, *The Ordeal of Power: A Political Memoir of the Eisenhower Years* (New York, 1963). A contrasting view of the administration is afforded by Stuart Gerry Brown, *Conscience in Politics: Adlai E. Stevenson in the 1950's* (Syracuse, 1961), and Bert Cochran, *Adlai Stevenson: Patrician among the Politicians* (New York, 1969).

Domestic legislation in the fifties and sixties is effectively analyzed in James L. Sundquist's *Politics and Policy: The Eisenhower, Kennedy, and Johnson Years* (Washington, 1968). Eisenhower's relations with his first Congress are examined in Gary W. Reichard's able monograph, *The Reaffirmation of Republicanism: Eisenhower and the Eighty-Third Congress* (Knoxville, 1975). The first "scandal" of the Eisenhower administration is considered in Aaron Wildavsky, *Dixon-Yates: A Study in Power Politics* (New Haven, 1962). For a broader view, see David A. Frier, *Conflict of Interest in the Eisenhower Administration* (Ames, Iowa, 1969).

John F. Kennedy's presidency is described in Theodore C. Sorensen's *Kennedy* (New York, 1965) and Arthur M. Schlesinger, jr.'s *A Thousand Days: John F. Kennedy in the White House* (Boston, 1965). Schlesinger's volume, a historian's memoir, chronicle, and commentary, catches the sweep and ferment of the thousand days. Aida DiPace Donald, ed., *John F. Kennedy and the New Frontier* (New York, 1966), contains appraisals of Kennedy's leadership, goals, and accomplishments. Henry Fairlie makes a critical assessment in *The Kennedy Promise: The Politics of Expectation* (New York, 1973). Other aspects of the Kennedy years are dealt with in Lawrence H. Fuchs, *John F. Kennedy and American Catholicism* (New York, 1967); William Manchester, *The Death of a President, November 20–November 26, 1963* (New York, 1967); and Edward Jay Epstein, *Inquest: The Warren Commission and the Establishment of Truth* (New York, 1966).

Journalistic accounts of the Johnson administration include Rowland Evans and Robert Novak, *Lyndon B. Johnson: The Exercise of Power, A Political Biography* (New York, 1966); Louis Heren, *No Hail, No Farewell* (New York, 1970); Richard Harwood and Haynes Johnson, *Lyndon* (New York, 1973); and Tom Wicker, *JFK and LBJ: The Influence of Personality upon Politics* (New York, 1968). Eric F. Goldman's *The Tragedy of Lyndon Johnson*

(New York, 1969) is a critical treatment by a disillusioned professor who served in the White House. For Johnson's own account, see *The Vantage Point: Perspectives of the Presidency, 1963–1969* (New York, 1971). Marvin E. Gettleman and David Mermelstein, eds., *The Great Society Reader: The Failure of American Liberalism* (New York, 1967), and John C. Donovan, *The Politics of Poverty* (New York, 1967), help explain the Great Society.

For contemporary introductions to the Nixon administration, see Rowland Evans, Jr. and Robert D. Novak, *Nixon in the White House: The Frustration of Power* (New York, 1972), and Garry Wills, *Nixon Agonistes: The Crisis of the Self-Made Man* (Boston, 1970). The story of the administration's abortive welfare reform program is told by Vincent J. Burke and Vee Burke in *Nixon's Good Deed: Welfare Reform* (New York, 1974). Key aspects of Nixonian politics, including the use of race, region, and "the social issue," are considered in Kevin P. Phillips, *The Emerging Republican Majority* (New York, 1969); Richard M. Scammon and Ben J. Wattenberg, *The Real Majority* (New York, 1970); and Reg Murphy and Hal Gulliver, *The Southern Strategy* (New York, 1971). Carl Bernstein and Bob Woodward, *All the King's Men* (New York, 1974), is a fascinating account of the Watergate cover-up and the role of the press in bringing it to light.

Several general histories cover postwar diplomacy and foreign policy. John W. Spanier's well-organized *American Foreign Policy since World War II* (4th ed.; New York, 1971) offers a broad survey from the realist perspective. Walter LaFeber's *America, Russia, and the Cold War, 1945–1971* (2d ed.; New York, 1972), a thoughtful and cogently argued interpretation stressing economic factors, is notably successful in relating domestic politics and foreign policy. Stephen E. Ambrose's *Rise to Globalism: American Foreign Policy since 1938* (Baltimore, 1971) is a lively and critical survey. In *The Faces of Power: Constancy and Change in United States Foreign Policy from Truman to Johnson* (New York, 1968), Seyom Brown compares the broad goals of the first four postwar presidents. The development of United States policy in Europe is described by Richard J. Barnet and Marcus G. Raskin, *After Twenty Years: Alternatives to the Cold War in Europe* (New York, 1965). For a valuable work on American policy in another part of the world, see Fred Greene, *U.S. Policy and the Security of Asia* (New York, 1968).

The annual volumes of *The United States in World Affairs,* prepared for the Council on Foreign Relations, are a convenient source of information on foreign affairs in the postwar period. A few of the many books that analyze foreign policy issues and agencies in our contemporary history are Ruth B. Russell, *The United Nations and United States Security Policy* (Washington, 1968); Amy M. Gilbert, *Executive Agreements and Treaties, 1946–1973: Framework of the Foreign Policy of the Period* (Endicott, N.Y., 1973); Robert E. Elder, *The Information Machine: The United States Information Agency and*

American Foreign Policy (Syracuse, 1968); Chalmers M. Roberts, *The Nuclear Years: The Arms Race and Arms Control, 1945–70* (New York, 1970); and Harry Howe Ransom, *The Intelligence Establishment* (Cambridge, Mass., 1970). The close linkage between domestic and foreign policy is revealed in an outstanding book by Bradford Westerfield, *Foreign Policy and Party Politics: Pearl Harbor to Korea* (New Haven, 1955). Samuel P. Huntington, *The Common Defense: Strategic Programs in National Politics* (New York, 1961), is an able analysis of military programs. Lawrence S. Wittner's *Rebels against War: The American Peace Movement, 1941–1960* (New York, 1969) suggests the extent to which the peace movement of the 1940s and 1950s connected the prewar Left and the New Left of the sixties.

The genesis of the cold war has had a peculiar fascination for American scholars. The best synthesis published thus far is John Lewis Gaddis, *The United States and the Origins of the Cold War, 1941–1947* (New York, 1972). Other important studies are Louis J. Halle, *The Cold War as History* (New York, 1967), and Herbert Feis, *From Trust to Terror: The Onset of the Cold War, 1945–1950* (New York, 1970). George C. Herring, Jr., *Aid to Russia, 1941–1946: Strategy, Diplomacy, the Origins of the Cold War* (New York, 1973), is a good monograph on the controversial issue of lend-lease. Most of these books were written from the liberal consensual viewpoint.

The 1960s brought a strong infusion of revisionism, including such books as David Horowitz, *The Free World Colossus: A Critique of American Foreign Policy in the Cold War* (New York, 1965); Lloyd C. Gardner, *Architects of Illusion: Men and Ideas in American Foreign Policy, 1941–1949* (Chicago, 1970); and Joyce Kolko and Gabriel Kolko, *The Limits of Power: The World and United States Foreign Policy, 1945–1954* (New York, 1972). The Kolkos argue that the goals of American foreign policy were dictated by institutional necessity. Central to all United States programs and policies following the war, they assert, was the determination "to restructure the world so that American business could trade, operate, and profit without restrictions everywhere." Thomas G. Paterson's *Soviet-American Confrontation: Postwar Reconstruction and the Origins of the Cold War* (Baltimore, 1973) is a solid study that dissents from both orthodox and revisionist interpretations. Critical evaluations of cold-war revisionism are made by Robert W. Tucker, *The Radical Left and American Foreign Policy* (Baltimore, 1971), and, more controversially, by Robert James Maddox, *The New Left and the Origins of the Cold War* (Princeton, 1973).

The major foreign policies of the postwar years are discussed in many of the administration accounts already mentioned in connection with domestic politics. Robert H. Ferrell's *George C. Marshall* (New York, 1966) and Gaddis Smith's *Dean Acheson* (New York, 1972), two volumes in the American Secretaries of State and Their Diplomacy series, are basic works on the Truman administration. Joseph M. Jones, *The Fifteen Weeks (February 21–June 5, 1947)* (New York, 1955), is an absorbing, inside account of the formulation of the Truman Doctrine and the Marshall Plan. Harry B. Price, *The Marshall Plan and Its Meaning* (Ithaca, 1955), and Robert Endicott Osgood, *NATO: The Entangling Alliance* (Chicago, 1962), are standard accounts. Richard F. Haynes, *The Awesome Power: Harry S. Truman as Commander in Chief* (Baton Rouge, 1973), describes the tremendous growth of presidential military power in the years after 1945.

The best studies of the Korean War are David Rees, *Korea: The Limited War* (New York, 1964), and John W. Spanier, *The Truman-MacArthur Controversy and the Korean War* (rev. ed.; New York, 1965). Other useful works on the Korean conflict are Glenn D. Paige, *The Korean Decision: June 24–30, 1950* (New York, 1968), and Allen S. Whiting, *China Crosses the Yalu: The Decision to Enter the Korean War* (New York, 1960). Ronald J. Caridi, *The Korean War and American Politics: The Republican Party as a Case Study* (Philadelphia, 1969), throws light on the domestic repercussions of the war.

The diplomacy of the Eisenhower era is outlined in David Bernard Capitanchik, *The Eisenhower Presidency and American Foreign Policy* (New York, 1969), and several books on the secretary of state, John Foster Dulles, the best of which are Louis L. Gerson, *John Foster Dulles* (New York, 1968), and Townsend Hoopes, *The Devil and John Foster Dulles* (Boston, 1973). Herman Finer's *Dulles over Suez: The Theory and Practice of His Diplomacy* (Chicago, 1964) is critical of Dulles's role. For the Eisenhower administration and Indochina, see Melvin Gurtov, *The First Vietnam Crisis: Chinese Communist Strategy and United States Involvement, 1953–1954* (New York, 1967). David Wise and Thomas B. Ross, *The U–2 Affair* (New York, 1962), is a journalistic account. Robert E. Osgood and others, *America and the World: From the Truman Doctrine to Vietnam* (Baltimore, 1970), is a series of thoughtful articles reappraising American foreign policy. Seymour Melman, *Pentagon Capitalism: The Political Economy of War* (New York, 1970), contends that significant changes took place in the military-industrial complex in the 1960s.

A good inside account of Kennedy's conduct of foreign affairs is Roger Hilsman, *To Move a Nation: The Politics of Foreign Policy in the Administration of John F. Kennedy* (New York, 1964). More critical assessments are offered by Richard J. Walton, *Cold War and Counterrevolution: The Foreign Policy of John F. Kennedy* (New York, 1972), and Louise FitzSimons, *The Kennedy Doctrine* (New York, 1972). The essence of the Kennedy doctrine, according to FitzSimons, was an "untenable globalism" that led to "increased areas of conflict, to a heightening of the arms race, and to American concern with and involvement . . . in the affairs of almost every

41

country of the world." Stephen Weissman, *American Foreign Policy in the Congo, 1960–1964* (Ithaca, 1974), is a good monograph for this period. Graham T. Allison's multiconceptual study, *Essence of Decision: Explaining the Cuban Missile Crisis* (Boston, 1971), views the Cuban missile confrontation as the touchstone of Kennedy's foreign policy and a "major watershed in the Cold War." See also Elie Abel, *The Missile Crisis* (Philadelphia, 1966).

A general treatment of the Johnson administration's foreign policies is provided in Philip L. Geyelin's *Lyndon B. Johnson and the World* (New York, 1966). David Halberstam's best seller, *The Best and the Brightest* (New York, 1972), is made up of sharply etched profiles of several key presidential advisers in the areas of strategy and diplomacy during the Kennedy and Johnson years. Johnson's intervention in the Dominican Republic is ably reviewed by Theodore Draper, *The Dominican Revolt: A Case Study in American Policy* (New York, 1968).

The literature on the United States in Vietnam is extensive. Frances FitzGerald, *Fire in the Lake: The Vietnamese and the Americans in Vietnam* (Boston, 1972), is distinctive for its sensitivity to Vietnamese politics and culture. George M. Kahin and John W. Lewis, *The United States in Vietnam* (rev. ed.; New York, 1969), is a good brief history. An outstanding description of policy making is made in Townsend Hoopes, *The Limits of Intervention: An Inside Account of How the Johnson Policy of Escalation in Vietnam Was Reversed* (New York, 1969). Hoopes's volume and Chester L. Cooper's *The Lost Crusade: America in Vietnam* (New York, 1970) provide examples of liberal dissent on the Vietnam question. More thoroughgoing revisionist critiques of U.S. policy in Vietnam include Noam Chomsky's *American Power and the New Mandarins* (New York, 1969) and Richard J. Barnet's *Roots of War* (New York, 1972).

The best available account of the Nixon administration's foreign policy is Henry Brandon's *The Retreat of American Power* (New York, 1973). The Nixon-Kissinger initiatives are also discussed in Robert E. Osgood and others, *Retreat from Empire? The First Nixon Administration* (Baltimore, 1973), and a number of books on Kissinger, including David Landau, *Kissinger: The Uses of Power* (Boston, 1972), and Marvin Kalb and Bernard Kalb, *Kissinger* (New York, 1974).

The struggle for Negro rights after the Second World War is incisively reviewed in C. Vann Woodward's history of racial segregation, *The Strange Career of Jim Crow* (3d rev. ed.; New York, 1974). A collaborative volume edited by Talcott Parsons and Kenneth B. Clark, *The Negro American* (Boston, 1966), undertakes a comprehensive survey of the problems and status of blacks in contemporary America. Charles E. Silberman's *Crisis in Black and White* (New York, 1964) is a wide-ranging journalistic treatment.

Harold R. Isaacs's *The New World of Negro Americans* (Cambridge, Mass., 1963) considers the way in which the rise of the new nonwhite nations affected the identity of black Americans. Anthony Lewis, *Portrait of a Decade: The Second American Revolution* (New York, 1964), is an outstanding piece of reporting, while Benjamin Muse, *The American Negro Revolution: From Nonviolence to Black Power, 1963–1967* (Bloomington, 1968), is a useful survey.

Two books review the first decade of the South's slow and tortuous accommodation to the school desegregation decision of 1954: Benjamin Muse, *Ten Years of Prelude: The Story of Integration since the Supreme Court's 1954 Decision* (New York, 1964), and Reed Sarratt, *The Ordeal of Desegregation: The First Decade* (New York, 1966). The desegregation process in later years is traced in Gary Orfield, *The Reconstruction of Southern Education: The Schools and the 1964 Civil Rights Act* (New York, 1969). The reaction of the South during the 1950s and early 1960s is analyzed in scholarly works by Numan V. Bartley, *The Rise of Massive Resistance: Race and Politics in the South during the 1950's* (Baton Rouge, 1969), and Neil R. McMillen, *The Citizens' Council: Organized Resistance to the Second Reconstruction, 1954–64* (Urbana, 1971). Hugh Davis Graham's *Crisis in Print: Desegregation and the Press in Tennessee* (Nashville, 1967) deals well with resistance in that state. I. A. Newby, *Challenge to the Court: Social Scientists and the Defense of Segregation, 1954–1966* (Baton Rouge, 1967), focuses on one line of resistance to racial change. An important study of black and white attitudes, based on much empirical data, is Donald R. Matthews and James W. Prothro, *Negroes and the New Southern Politics* (New York, 1966). Chandler Davidson's *Biracial Politics: Conflict and Coalition in the Metropolitan South* (Baton Rouge, 1972) is a first-rate study of black political involvement at the grass-roots level, in this instance Houston. A classic interpretation of the most race-haunted state in the Union is given in James W. Silver, *Mississippi: The Closed Society* (rev. ed.; New York, 1966).

The best biography of Martin Luther King, Jr. is David L. Lewis, *King: A Critical Biography* (New York, 1970). But see also King's own *Stride toward Freedom: The Montgomery Story* (New York, 1958) and *Why We Can't Wait* (New York, 1964). One of King's campaigns is described in Charles E. Fager, *Selma, 1965: The Town Where the South Was Changed* (New York, 1974). August Meier and Elliott Rudwick, *CORE: A Study in the Civil Rights Movement, 1942–1968* (New York, 1973), is the most authoritative history yet written of a postwar civil rights organization. Howard Zinn's *SNCC: The New Abolitionists* (2d ed.; Boston, 1965) is a more impressionistic account written by a participant. Racial discrimination and black protest in other parts of the country are treated in Louis E. Lomax, *The Negro Revolt* (New York, 1962); James Q. Wilson, *Negro Politics: The Search for Leadership*

(Glencoe, 1960); and William A. Osborne, *The Segregated Covenant: Race Relations and American Catholics* (New York, 1967). Lee Rainwater and William L. Yancey, *The Moynihan Report and the Politics of Controversy* (Cambridge, Mass., 1967), reprints Daniel Patrick Moynihan's famous study of the black family and some of the reactions to it.

Three personal accounts are helpful in understanding the coalescing mood of black militancy and black nationalism in the 1960s: James Baldwin, *The Fire Next Time* (New York, 1963); Eldridge Cleaver, *Soul on Ice* (New York, 1968); and Malcolm Little, with the assistance of Alex Haley, *The Autobiography of Malcolm X* (New York, 1965). C. Eric Lincoln, *The Black Muslims in America* (Boston, 1961), and E. U. Essien-Udom, *Black Nationalism: A Search for an Identity in America* (Chicago, 1962), are standard works. The riots of the 1960s are analyzed in Robert M. Fogelson, *Violence as Protest: A Study of Riots and Ghettos* (Garden City, 1971). Robert Conot's *Rivers of Blood, Years of Darkness* (New York, 1967) is a popular account of the Watts riot of 1965. Hugh Davis Graham and Ted Robert Gurr, *Violence in America: Historical and Comparative Perspectives* (Washington, 1969), is a comprehensive historical and sociological work.

The new feminism, like the black renaissance, has become the subject of much investigation and a growing body of literature in recent years. Excellent historical background is provided by William Henry Chafe's *The American Woman: Her Changing Social, Economic, and Political Roles, 1920–1970* (New York, 1972). The new ideology of the 1960s, Chafe argues, was the result of significant behavioral changes in the role of women brought about by World War II. Betty Friedan, *The Feminine Mystique* (New York, 1963), is a good source for the history of women in the 1950s, while Judith Hole and Ellen Levine, *Rebirth of Feminism* (New York, 1971), is valuable for the emergence of the movement to eliminate sexism in the 1960s.

A good place to begin the study of the urban revolution and the crisis of the city in contemporary America is Zane L. Miller's *The Urbanization of Modern America: A Brief History* (New York, 1973) and Sam Bass Warner's *The Urban Wilderness: A History of the American City* (New York, 1972). Daniel J. Elazar, *Cities of the Prairie: The Metropolitan Frontier and American Politics* (New York, 1970), illuminates the rapid metropolitanization of one region in the years following World War II. Different historical approaches to two American cities are revealed in Roy Lubove, *Twentieth-Century Pittsburgh: Government, Business, and Environmental Change* (New York, 1969), and Stephan Thernstrom, *The Other Bostonians: Poverty and Progress in the American Metropolis, 1880–1970* (Cambridge, Mass., 1973). In *The Emerging City: Myth and Reality* (New York, 1962) Scott A. Greer considers the leadership, governance, and distribution of power in American cities. Jane Jacobs offers a sharp critique of modern urban culture and the work of urban planners in *The Death and Life of Great American Cities* (New York, 1961). Among the best books on the urban crisis and the efforts to revitalize the city are Scott A. Greer, *Urban Renewal and American Cities: The Dilemma of Democratic Intervention* (Indianapolis, 1966); Jeanne R. Lowe, *Cities in a Race with Time: Progress and Poverty in America's Renewing Cities* (New York, 1967); and Daniel Patrick Moynihan, ed., *Toward a National Urban Policy* (New York, 1970).

Various aspects of suburbanization are dealt with in Robert C. Wood, *Suburbia: Its People and Their Politics* (Boston, 1959); William M. Dobriner, *Class in Suburbia* (Englewood Cliffs, 1963); Herbert J. Gans, *The Levittowners: Ways of Life and Politics in a New Suburban Community* (New York, 1967); and Scott Donaldson, *The Suburban Myth* (New York, 1969). Clarence S. Stein's *Toward New Towns for America* (Cambridge, Mass., 1957) is a historical and pictorial interpretation of the "new town" movement in the twentieth century by a participant.

In the related area of environmental problems a convenient introduction is available in John Opie, ed., *Americans and Environment: The Controversy over Ecology* (Lexington, Mass., 1971). Among the helpful books dealing with the environmental movement are Robert Rienow and Leona Train Rienow, *Moment in the Sun: A Report on the Deteriorating Quality of the American Environment* (New York, 1967); Frank Graham, *Since Silent Spring* (Boston, 1970), an absorbing account of the reaction to Rachel Carson's book *Silent Spring* (1962); John C. Esposito, *Vanishing Air: The Ralph Nader Study Group Report on Air Pollution* (New York, 1970); J. Clarence Davies, III, *The Politics of Pollution* (New York, 1970), which focuses on the policy process; and Robert Disch, ed., *The Ecological Conscience: Values for Survival* (Englewood Cliffs, 1970), on the nature and ethical aspects of the problem. S. David Freeman, *Energy: The New Era* (New York, 1974), explores the origins of the fuel crisis of the 1970s and offers a blueprint for future action.

The dimensions of the cultural crisis of the sixties and seventies are suggested in Theodore Roszak, *The Making of a Counter Culture* (Garden City, 1969); Charles A. Reich, *The Greening of America* (New York, 1970); Lewis S. Feuer, *The Conflict of Generations: The Character and Significance of Student Movements* (New York, 1969); Alvin Toffler, *Future Shock* (New York, 1970); Philip E. Slater, *The Pursuit of Loneliness: American Culture at the Breaking Point* (Boston, 1970); and Patricia Cayo Sexton and Brendan Sexton, *Blue Collars and Hard Hats: The Working Class and the Future of American Politics* (New York, 1971). In such books as *The Uncommitted: Alienated Youth in American Society* (New York, 1965) and *Young Radicals: Notes on Committed Youth* (New York, 1968) Kenneth Keniston suggests that rebels and deviants often furnish invaluable indexes to the central problems of a culture. Seymour Martin Lipset, *Rebellion in the University* (Boston, 1972), is a splendid analysis of student radicalism. Kirkpatrick Sale's *SDS* (New York, 1973) is a detailed account of the Students for a Democratic Society. Laurence R. Veysey, *The Communal Experience: Anarchist and Mystical Counter-Cultures in America* (New York, 1973), is a study in cultural radicalism that concentrates on a number of selected communes. See also Ron E. Roberts, *The New Communes: Coming Together in America* (Englewood Cliffs, 1971).

The revival of radicalism in the sixties is ably described by Irwin Unger in *The Movement: A History of the American New Left, 1959–1972* (New York, 1974). John P. Diggins, *The American Left in the Twentieth Century* (New York, 1973), explores the social origins, ideologies, and historical contexts of three distinct American lefts, including the new radicalism of the 1960s. Radical social thought and the phenomenon of the New Left are also examined by Christopher Lasch, *The Agony of the American Left* (New York, 1969); Richard King, *The Party of Eros: Radical Social Thought and the Realm of Freedom* (Chapel Hill, 1972); Peter Clecak, *Radical Paradoxes: Dilemmas of the American Left, 1945–1970* (New York, 1973); and Edward J. Bacciocco, Jr., *The New Left in America: Reform to Revolution, 1956–1970* (Stanford, 1974).